Tudor *Homes*

Tony D. Triggs

This book is dedicated to my daughter, Donna

ACKNOWLEDGEMENTS

The author and publishers would like to thank the following for permission to reproduce photographs and other material:

Andy Bailey	24 (left)
Bodleian Library, Oxford	11 (bottom)
The Bridgeman Art Library Ltd.	cover; 36; 37 (top); 42
The Bridgeman Art Library and Burghley House, Stamford, Lincs.	33 (left); 37 (bottom)
The Bridgeman Art Library and Belvoir Castle, Leicestershire	19 (bottom right)
The Bridgeman Art Library and Trinity College, Cambridge	20 (bottom)
The Bridgeman Art Library and Frick Collection	30
The British Film Institute, Still, Posters and Designs and Columbia Films	31
By permission of The British Library	8 (bottom)
N. Cooke © T.D. Triggs	8 (top)
Edinburgh University Library	17 (right)
The Golden Hind	43 (top)
English Heritage	14; 25; 26; 38 (top), (bottom) (Ivan Lapper); 47
The Hulton Deutson Collection	34 (bottom)
Kentwell Hall	5
Leicestershire Museums, Arts and Records Services	11 (top)
Mansell Collection	15; 17; 23 (top)
By kind permission of the Marquess of Tavistock and the Trustees of the Bedford Estates	34 (top)
Mary Evans Picture Library	16; 18; 19 (top); 28 (top)
National Maritime Museum Publications	40; 44
Christine Moorcroft	24 (right); 25
By courtesy of The National Portrait Gallery, London	19 (bottom); 32; 47 (left)
The National Trust	46 (left) (Mike Cadwell)
Reproduced from the (1992) Ordnance Survey 1:25 000 map with the permission of the Controller of H.M.S.O. ©	10
Shakespeare Centre Library: Thos. F. and Mig Holte Collection	46 (right)
Ronald Sheridan/Ancient Art and Architecture Collection	title; 9; 12; 13; 20 (top); 21; 22; 23 (bottom); 29 (bottom)
The Royal Collect © Her Majesty the Queen	33
Science Photo Library	22 (top right)
The Wellcome Institute Library, London	22 (top left)
Westminster Cathedral and Weidenfeld & Nicolson Archives	29

The publishers have made every effort to contact copyright holders but this has not always been possible. If any have been overlooked we will be pleased to make any necessary arrangements.

First published 1992 as *Primary History: Tudor and Stuart Times* by Folens Limited, Albert House, Apex Business Centre, Boscombe Road, Dunstable LU5 4RL, England. Revised edition published 1995.

ISBN 1 8527821-5

Cover Design: Design for Marketing, Ware.

Editor: Caroline Arthur.

Printed in Singapore by Craft Print Pte Ltd.

Illustrators: Peter Dennis of Linda Rogers Associates.

Layout artist: Patricia Hollingsworth.

CONTENTS

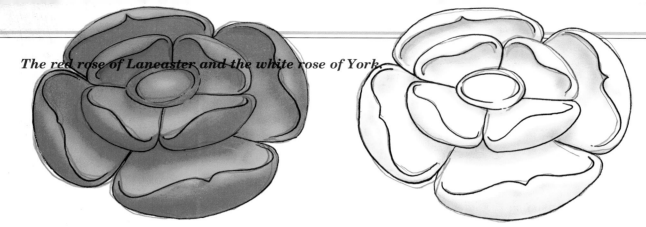
The red rose of Lancaster and the white rose of York.

Stripped of its armour and clothing, torn by wounds and covered with mud, the dead king's body was thrown on to an old horse ...

1. The Wars of the Roses

The words at the top of the page were written just after the Battle of Bosworth in 1485. The dead king was Richard III; the winner of the battle was Prince Henry Tudor. Henry Tudor took Richard's place as King of England and Wales. He became Henry VII.

For 30 years before the Battle there had been gang warfare in England as two branches of the royal family fought for power. One branch was known as the House of Lancaster and the other was known as the House of York. Each side had a rose on its banner or badge, so the wars are called the Wars of the Roses.

Both sides had very powerful supporters. These included the barons – men who owned huge amounts of land. The barons controlled the lives of the men and women who lived on their land, and could order the men to fight on their side. It was hard for a monarch to destroy the barons who fought against him or her.

 Someone said of Richard III shortly after he died:

He was small of body and weak in strength but he most bravely defended himself as a noble knight to his last breath. He was killed fighting manfully in the thick of his enemies.

 **Richard III.
What sort of man?**

Look again at the things that were written about Richard shortly after he died.

1. Do you think the writers liked him or not?
2. Whose soldiers took his body from the battlefield? Why do you think so?

The Battle of Bosworth was the last battle in the Wars of the Roses. The new king, Henry VII, brought the Wars to an end. Here are some clues about Henry VII's character:

- He belonged to the House of Lancaster but he chose a wife from the House of York: Elizabeth.
- When he captured a youth pretending to be a rival prince, he spared his life and gave him a job in his kitchens.

The roses

Look at the rose designs used by the House of Lancaster and the House of York. Then look at the rose in the courtyard of Kentwell Hall.

1. Why do you think the red and white roses have been put together at Kentwell Hall?
2. When do you think people started to use the Tudor Rose?
3. Why do you think they invented it?

Henry VII. What sort of man?

Discuss the clues about Henry VII.

1. What sort of person do you think he was?

Key ideas

baron	power
emblem	warfare

Kentwell Hall.

Henry VII reigned 1485–1509.

Married Elizabeth of York 1486.

The rose both red and white
In one rose now doth grow.

2. The Tudors

The son of Henry VII and Elizabeth of York became Henry VIII. He married a woman called Catherine of Aragon, who gave birth to a daughter, Mary. Henry wanted a son to take his place when he died. When Catherine got too old to have any more children, Henry divorced her and married a younger woman called Anne Boleyn.

Henry and Anne had a daughter, Elizabeth, but Henry was now desperate to have a son. He had Anne beheaded and married for a third time. His new wife, Jane Seymour, died a year later – soon after giving birth to a son, Edward.

Henry married three more times but he had no more children.

Henry VIII reigned 1509–1547.

Key ideas

monarch
succession

Henry VIII

1. How many of Henry VIII's children became monarchs?
2. In what order did they reign?
3. Why was Henry desperate for a son?

Mary I reigned 1553–1558.

? Succession

1. What rules about age and sex were used to settle the order in which Henry's children reigned?

Royal family

1. Find out the order in which members of the present Royal Family will reign.
2. Are the same rules used as in Tudor times?
3. If your family were royal, who would be the next monarch?

Married Catherine of Aragon 1510.

Henry VIII's wives

Married Anne Boleyn 1533.

Married Jane Seymour 1536.

Married Anne of Cleves 1539.

Married Catherine Howard 1540.

Married Catherine Parr 1543.

Elizabeth I reigned 1558–1603.

Edward VI reigned 1547–1553.

Hark, hark,
The dogs do bark,
The beggars are coming
to town;
Some in rags,
Some in jags
And one in a velvet gown.

3. Life in the Country

In the 16th century most people lived in villages and they never saw a town in their lives. Their wooden homes were like giant huts. There was just one room in the hut, with a floor of bare earth and a fire in the middle for cooking and warmth. These, unlike some of the homes of the rich, have not survived to the present day.

B *This Tudor farmhouse in West Yorkshire was built from wood and the roof was thatched. Stone walls and tiles were added in the 17th century.*

Key ideas

common land   export

Roofs were usually thatched with straw. Smoke from the fire escaped through the thatch and through cracks and small windows, which had no glass. Only the rich could afford to have glass.

A *A picture from a Tudor manuscript*

The homes and work of country people

1. Very few poor people's homes have survived from Tudor times. Explain how the farmhouse in Source **B** has survived.
2. Villagers sometimes coated wooden buildings with clay. Why do you think they did this?
3. Cottages had little furniture. What do you think people slept on?
4. Sources **A** and **C** show some jobs done by country people. Describe what they are doing.

Nowadays, most of our food comes from shops. There is plenty of it and few people bother to grow their own. In Tudor times, most people had to grow food or they would have starved. They had herbs and vegetables in their gardens and crops and animals in their fields. There might be corn in one field, peas in another and sheep in a third. They used the sheep's wool to make themselves clothes. There was rarely any wool or cloth left over to sell.

Life could be very hard for the villagers. Often the local miller charged too much for grinding their grain into flour. Sometimes he kept some flour for himself, leaving the villagers hungry. They also went hungry whenever bad weather ruined their crops.

Life became even harder when rich people started to keep more sheep. Unlike the cottagers, they could earn money by selling cloth abroad – it was England's main export. They stopped letting poor people use the land – sometimes by raising the rents so high that no one could pay them. They even began to fence in commons (land that people had always shared). The commons, too, became part of the new, gigantic sheep farms.

 A hard life

Imagine you are a villager in Tudor times.

1. Write a letter to a friend in a town describing your worries.

C *A picture from Tudor times*

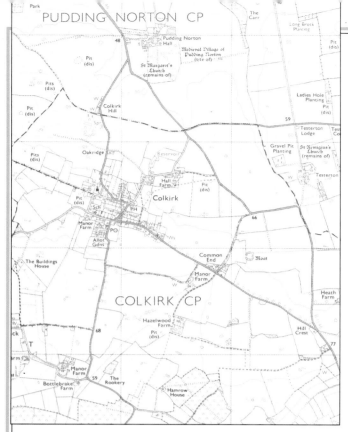

D *A modern map of the Colkirk area in Norfolk*

Key idea

enclosure

Fencing in land for sheep was called enclosure. It left the poor with less land on which to grow their food, and food was often too expensive to buy.

In 1552, a leaflet by an unknown author summed up the poor folks' problems in the following way:

The more sheep, the dearer is the wool.
The more sheep, the dearer is the mutton.
The more sheep, the dearer is the beef.
The more sheep, the dearer is the corn.
The more sheep, the scanter (scarcer) is the white meat (butter and cheese).
The more sheep, the fewer eggs for a penny.

The leaflet went on to explain how things had been in the past:

It was far better when there was not only enough sheep, but also oxen, cows, pigs, geese and chickens, eggs, butter and cheese – yes, and bread, corn, and malt besides, and all produced on the same land.

Lately, I have heard of a dozen ploughs – all of them less than six miles from here – abandoned in the last seven years; and where 40 people had their living, now there is just one man and his shepherd.

What happened to all the country folk who had to give up their ploughs and their homes? Many were forced to go begging in towns. Soon the few towns that existed were full of beggars. The citizens felt they were being invaded.

Some Tudor villages lost all their people and were never rebuilt. Other villages did not die out, but the wooden homes were replaced with new ones of brick or stone. Many modern villages and towns stand on the sites of these Tudor villages.

Local history

What can you find out about an area near where you live in Tudor times? Libraries may be helpful.

1. Compare a map from Tudor times with a present-day map. Draw your own map and mark on it any villages that have disappeared.
2. Have any villages grown into towns?
3. Use local history books and aerial photographs to find out about how the land was used in Tudor times.
   What have you learned about your local area in Tudor times?

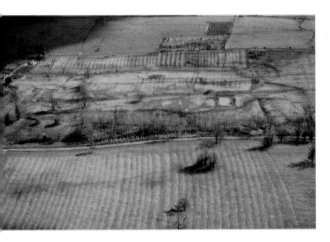

This photograph shows that tracks and houses can leave patterns in the ground. Ploughing often smooths them out, but the drawing below shows that the pattern can reappear in a field of growing crops. This is because the depth of the soil affects their height.

Enclosure and poverty

Think about the changes in the countryside.

1. Look at Source **D**. Can you see any signs of villages that have disappeared?
2. 'Sheep eat up men.' What do you think people meant by this in Tudor times?
3. The rhyme at the start of the chapter is from Tudor times. It tells us the sort of thing that happened but it may not be exactly true.
   Do you think any beggars might have been seen in velvet gowns? Why do you think so?

The hunt for food

1. Pretend that you live in a town in Tudor times and discuss how you feel about country people who come begging for food or asking for work.

Windsor attracted many people and began to turn into a small town. This was partly because the castle there needed many workers. This map was drawn in the early 17th century.

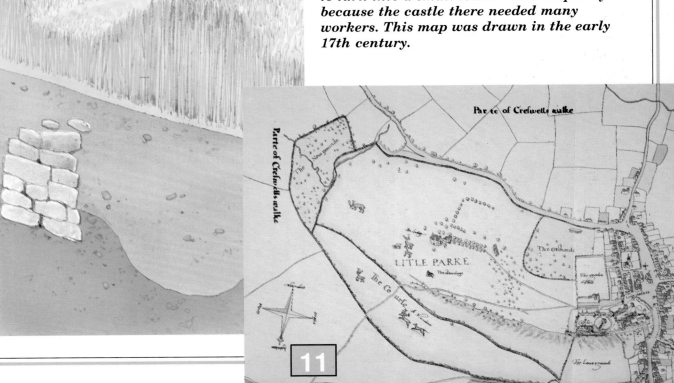

Wales had once been a separate country but the English had conquered it, treating it like a part of England.

Many of the people were sheep farmers living high up in the hills. They turned the sheep's wool into clothes for themselves and they also sold cloth to English merchants. Sometimes the English treated the Welsh unfairly, making them sell their cloth to English merchants at very low prices.

The Welsh also sold coal, metal and stone mined from their mountains. Like farming, mining was usually done by families. Sometimes the miners found the coal and rock at the surface, but usually they had to dig pits. There might be two men chipping away at the coal or rock with axes and putting the pieces into a barrel. Other men then had to haul the full barrel out of the pit.

B *Welsh villagers working in a coal mine*

?

Work and trade

1. Look at Source **A**. Describe the goods that the Welsh imported and exported.
2. Wool was in great demand in England and Wales, but Welsh sheep farmers did not become rich. Why not?
3. Describe the work shown in Source **B**.

A *A map to show trade and industry in Wales*

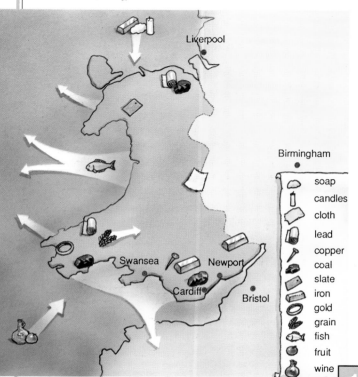

soap
candles
cloth
lead
copper
coal
slate
iron
gold
grain
fish
fruit
wine

Transporting coal and other goods was difficult because of the mountains. Wealthy people burnt coal to keep warm, but they bought it from mines very near their homes. Stone and coal from mines near the sea were carried by boat, and Wales had some very busy ports.

Key ideas

conquer   leisure
export   merchant
import

These Tudor archers are using crossbows.

Games

Read the description of games played in Tudor times.

1. Men *had* to practise with bows and arrows. Why do you think this was important?

Read Thomas Elyot's description of a ball game and the descriptions of other violent games.

2. Elyot said that the ball game should be banned, but this did not happen. It has developed into two modern games. Can you think what they are?
3. Some wrestlers wore hard shoes. Try to think of a reason for this.

Even the poor had some time for leisure. Village youths played a very rough ball game: they formed two teams then they fought their way across the countryside, with each team trying to get the ball to a different place – an inn, perhaps.

A Tudor writer called Sir Thomas Elyot wrote about the players' injuries:

Sometimes their necks are broken, sometimes their backs, sometimes their legs, sometimes their arms ... (The game) is nothing but beastly fury and extreme violence.

Archery became a popular outdoor sport for both rich and poor. The targets set up in a field were called butts. (We still use the word when we say that someone is the butt or target of an unkind joke. The word 'butt' is also used in the names of some roads or districts.)

While the poor shot at targets, the rich went hunting. There were royal forests that were full of deer and other game. Hunting was often followed by feasting.

Other violent games included fighting with sticks, boxing and wrestling. Rich people also enjoyed sword fights and jousting.

Local History

What can you find out from local guide books, local history books, maps and records from courts and libraries?

1. Is there a road or district near where you live that has 'butt' in its name. What might have happened there in Tudor times?
   You could look at street guides and maps.
2. Find out about trade and industry in your area. Which trades or industries could date from Tudor times? Look for clues to support your ideas.

In every street carts and coaches make such a thundering. Hammers are beating, pots clinking ... porters sweating under burdens, and merchants carrying bags of money.

4. Town Life

Most towns in Tudor times were very small. The smell of dung and hay from the fields must have mixed with the smell of bread baking in people's ovens.

London was the only really large town. By the end of Queen Elizabeth's reign it had 120 churches and a maze of busy, crowed streets. Alleys leading off the streets were sometimes so narrow that people pushing carts did not have room to pass. The overhanging upper storeys shut out most of the light and air.

 According to a writer called John Stow, who wrote *A Survey of London* in 1598:

The number of ... carts and coaches must needs be dangerous ... The coachman rides behind the horse tails (and) lashes them (although) the forehorse of every carriage should be led by hand.

Farmers sometimes drove cattle through the streets to market. Butchers bought the cattle and drove them to their shops, where they killed them and cut them up for sale.

Each trade had its own street or district. Butchers gathered in one place and people who sold poultry gathered somewhere else. In 1500 there were said to be 52 goldsmiths' shops in a single street.

Streets or districts were named after the trades that were carried on there. Part of London is still called Poultry, and streets called Shambles get their name from the tables used for butchering meat.

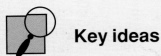

Key ideas

merchant   trade

Tudor town houses in Norwich

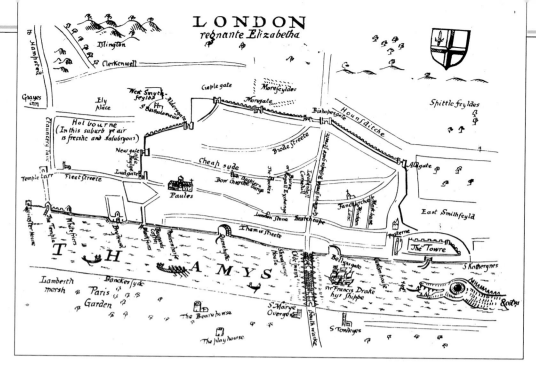

A map of London from the time of Elizabeth I

Streets and traders

1. Compare how meat got to shops in Tudor times and how it gets to shops today. Explain this difference.
2. Why do you think Tudor traders gathered in separate streets or districts?
3. Try to find some street names in your own town that show what trade once went on there. Is it still carried on? If not, try to explain what has changed.

An Italian visitor called Alessandro Magno described houses in London.

First, they construct a frame of wood, joined together with wooden pegs, and then between one layer of wood and another they put bricks ... Inside, the houses are ... decorated with wood carving. On the floors they put straw which they change often as a protection against the damp. Near the windows and around the rooms there are dishes for flowers and sweet-smelling herbs ... For wall coverings they use many tapestries woven with leaves, flowers and beautiful ... designs.

When people died, friends often made inventories of the things in their homes. The inventory for a man called John Port shows that his home had a tapestry in nearly every room.

London in the reign of Elizabeth

1. Study the map and list any place names connected with trades.
2. List any features and districts that still survive.
3. Describe what a pedestrian would see, smell and hear while walking from Gray's Inn to the Bear House.

Comfort and wealth

1. How can we tell from the passage that London was full of unpleasant smells? What do you think caused them?
2. Would Alessandro Magno have stayed with poor folk or wealthy folk? How does this affect what he says about Londoners having tapestries and bowls of flowers?

A rat-catcher's chant:

Rats or mice, have you any rats, mice, polecats or weasels,
Or have you any old sows sick of the measles?
I can kill them, and I can kill moles, and I can kill vermin
That creep up and creep down, and peep into holes!

A rat-catcher in London. Killing rats and other vermin was a full time job for dozens of people. They called out to let people know they were there.

Public health

1. List all the things that made London unhealthy in Tudor times. In each case say how conditions are different nowadays.
2. Say how the two accounts of London's new water system differ and suggest the reason.
3. Do you think the water came from the part of the River upstream of London or downstream of London? Why do you think so?

The Tudors tried to solve the problems of dirt and disease. In 1563 London's Mayor and council ordered that 'the filthy dunghill lying in the highway near unto Finsbury Court be removed and carried away' They also ordered the inhabitants not to make a new heap!

Few houses had toilets. Some people had a garden in which they could dig a hole; others poured their slops into gutters which emptied into the River Thames. Homes and palaces by the river did have toilets, which also emptied into the River. Downstream, the river must have been filthy but upstream it was 'most charming and quite full of swans white as snow.'

Londoners had always carried water from wells, streams or the River Thames. By the end of Queen Elizabeth's reign, arrangements for getting water were changing. According to *The Annals of England* by John Stow:

This year (1580) ... a most ingenious gentleman set up an engine ... to convey Thames water up into the city, sufficient to serve the whole west part thereof, being conveyed into men's houses by pipes of lead.

Twelve years later, someone called Joseph Rathgeb gave a slightly different account:

The ... water is preserved in various parts of the city, in large well-built stone cisterns, to be drawn off by cocks, and the poor water-bearers carry it on their shoulders to the different houses and sell it in a peculiar kind of wooden vessel, broad at the bottom but very narrow at the top and bound with iron hoops.

Paremptitius

A water carrier

By the end of Queen Elizabeth's reign London was growing rapidly. The centre was becoming more crowded, with buildings squeezed in everywhere, and London was also spreading into the countryside.

Cockpits were places where people watched cockerels or other birds tearing each other to pieces.

 In 1603, John Stow described how Hog Lane had changed:

Within these forty years (it) had on both sides fair hedgerows of elm trees with bridges and easy stiles to pass over into the pleasant fields, (where) citizens (could) walk, shoot and otherwise recreate and refresh their dull spirits in the sweet and wholesome air.

(It) is now within a few years made a continual building throughout, of garden houses and small cottages; and the fields on either side be turned into garden plots, tenter yards, bowling alleys and such like.

 Key idea

recreation

 Work and recreation

1. Find out what 'tenter yards' were.
2. What do you think 'bowling alleys' were like?
3. Describe other ways in which Londoners enjoyed themselves.
4. Would modern people object to some of the Tudors' pastimes? Write a conversation or argument in which they discuss them and argue about them.

5. Henry VIII

Here is a description of Henry aged about 30:

His Majesty is very handsome and very well built. He has got a beard that looks like gold. He is good at music, an excellent horseman and clever with words. He has prayers three times a day when he hunts and five times a day when he stays at home.

Here is a description of Henry as a teenager:

His majesty is the handsomest prince I ever set eyes on; taller than usual and with very fine legs. His skin is light and glowing and he has reddish brown hair which is straight and short in the French style. His chubby face is so beautiful that it would suit a pretty woman. He speaks French, English, Latin and a little Italian; he plays well on the lute and harpsichord, and can sing a piece of music as soon as he sees the page. He draws a bow with greater strength than any man in England and jousts marvellously.

Key ideas

evidence   monarch

A *A portrait of Henry in 1526, when he was 35*

What people said about Henry VIII

1. What do both quotations say about Henry VIII?
2. Find ways in which the quotations differ. Explain these differences.
3. What sort of things do the quotations not tell you about Henry?
4. How could people find out these things?

Portraits of Henry VIII

Look at the portraits of Henry on these two pages.

1. Written sources tell us that Henry had scars on his face, but the pictures do not show them. Why do you think this is?
2. What can you tell from the portraits about Henry's interests?
3. What does Source **D** tell us about how Henry wanted people to think of him? Explain your answer.
4. Describe Henry's clothes and jewellery.
5. Why do you think he chose these clothes and jewellery to wear for his portraits?

Compare the portraits with the quotations.

6. What similarities can you find?
7. Describe any differences.
8. Why do you think monarchs have portraits painted?

C *Henry was keen on music. This picture shows him playing a type of harp.*

Evidence from portraits

1. How are photographs different from painted portraits?
2. Compare two types of photographs of today's Royal Family: posed portraits and news report photographs.
3. Do you think photographs always show people as they really are?

B ▲ *A portrait of Henry when he was in his fifties*

D *Henry VIII painted by Holbein* ▶

6. New Ideas and Lands

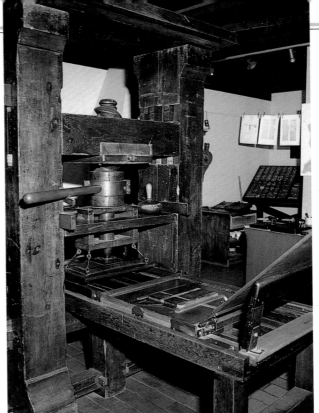

Gutenberg's printing press, about 1460.

Books had always been copied out by hand in monasteries, and the Church had controlled the spread of ideas by deciding which books the monks and nuns should copy and which they should burn.

In Henry VIII's time, good ways of printing were being invented. The printing machines (called presses) were owned by private individuals and not by the Church. Copying out a book by hand could take a year; a printer could turn out hundreds of copies within a few months. Often, the books were completely new, not just copies of old ones, and some of them said things the Church disliked.

- The Church said that the sun and the stars go round the earth.
- Scientists (like Galileo) proved that the earth goes round the sun.
- Anatomists (like Vesalius) defied the Church and cut up dead bodies to study the organs.
- People soon learned that the world was round (not flat as the Church had always taught) and they heard about newly-discovered continents.

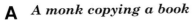

A *A monk copying a book*

Printing

Look at the pictures of the monk copying a book and Gutenberg's printing press.

1. How did the Church stop people finding out about new ideas?
2. What new ideas were there?
3. Think of two reasons why the invention of printing changed this.

A 15th century map of the world

Key ideas

colony
exploration
industry
medicine
slavery

Explorers thought that if the world was round they could sail west from Europe to get to Asia. Instead, they came to North and South America – whole continents they had never heard of.

Christopher Columbus sailed from Spain in 1492. He was one of the first explorers to reach America. He and the native people must have been very surprised to see each other.

 Here are some of the things Columbus wrote about the natives:

I gave some of them red caps, glass beads and many other little things, and they brought us parrots and balls of cotton and spears and many other things.

They would make fine servants, and when I leave I will bring back half a dozen of them. With fifty men we could overcome all the natives and make them do what we wanted. We could take them to Spain or make them slaves on their own land.

Old and New Worlds

1. Why do you think the native people did not write anything about Columbus?
2. What do you think people from Europe were planning to do with the natives' land? (Columbus' last few words should give you a very good clue.)
3. What does Source **A** tell you about how the explorers thought of the natives?
4. How is the 15th century map of the world different from one modern map on page 41?
5. What does this tell you about what people knew in the 15th century?

A *Columbus discovers America.*

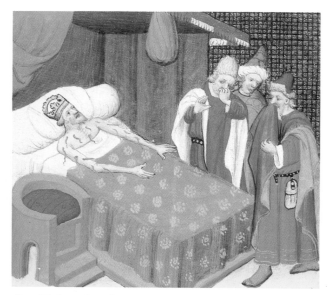

A *Using leeches*

B *Using cupping glasses. A picture from Paracelsus's book on anatomy, written in 1565.*

In Henry VIII's time, people thought many illnesses were caused by having too much blood. Doctors and barbers let out blood by cutting the patient and placing blood-sucking leeches on the body or scratching the skin and using a heated 'cupping glass'.

Old hand-written books about medicine described treatment such as bleeding, an idea that went back over 1,000 years. These books also said that constellations or groups of stars 'ruled' parts of the body and how the blood circulated.

Herbal remedies were very popular. People believed that a plant existed to cure every illness and they sometimes chose the plant according to what it looked like. For example, to cure a liver disease they might choose a plant with liver-shaped leaves.

Bleeding

1. Look at Sources **A** and **B**. What is happening to the people? Explain why.
2. Look at Source **C**. Some barbers still have striped poles outside their shops. Explain what this sign might stand for.

C *A barber's shop dating from Tudor times.*

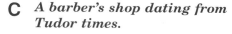

Key ideas

medicine   mortality

The title page to Andreas Vesalius' major work on the structure of the human body.

 In 1527 an anatomist called Paracelsus said:

Patients are the only books.

 Anatomy

1. How did Paracelsus think doctors should find out about their patients?
2. How did Vesalius find out about how the human body works?
3. Doctors and scholars before the 16th century rarely dissected dead bodies. Why do you think this was?

 Finding out

Compare Michelangelo's painting with earlier paintings of people.

1. How is it different? Explain how he was able to paint human bodies so realistically.

However, people were learning not to trust books automatically, but to find things out by experiment and observation. Ideas about the body changed rapidly as Vesalius and other anatomists dissected dead bodies. Treatments changed too, but experience showed that some herbal medicines worked very well. Modern pills and medicines still use substances that are found in plants, although they are sometimes made artificially.

Michelangelo, an Italian artist, dissected bodies to find out about bones and muscles.

A painting by Michelangelo

Do not try any of these medicines. They may be harmful.

Age 20   30

 Smallpox

 Malaria: attacks of shivering

Head injury in a jousting contest

 Ulcer on leg

 Becoming fat

Smallpox was sometimes treated with 'tea' made from holly leaves.

Fevers or attacks of shivering were treated with feverfew.
The name of the plant means 'Fever Cure'.

These plants were used to treat many illnesses.
They can still be seen growing wild or in gardens.

Calendula or marigold.

Vervain or verbena.

 Key ideas

medicine
mortality

Health Time Line

Key

 Illness or injury that affected Henry for the rest of his life.

40   50   56

 Serious head injury in a jousting contest: headaches

 Ulcers on both legs

 Blood clot on lung? Problems with breathing

 Difficulty walking and climbing stairs

Death

Injuries were sometimes treated with periwinkle or its juice. Bad wounds were sometimes kept open with small linen plugs so that bloody pus could drain out.

Ulcers were sometimes covered with poultices, (pastes made from leaves and clay). Mouldy bread was sometimes used in poultices.

Servants used a machine to lift Henry upstairs.

 ## Illnesses and remedies

1. Which of Henry's illnesses and injuries still affect people in Britain today? Why do some no longer occur?
2. Discuss how modern treatments differ from those used in Tudor times.

3. Find out the average age of death in Britain today. Why do you think most people live longer than Henry did? (There are many reasons.)

The Church had always claimed that what it taught and did was based on the Bible. In the early 16th century, churches all over Europe got their own printed Bibles, and priests and scholars began to point out mistakes which the Church had made. (Only priests and scholars could read the Bible because it was written in Latin.) This led to changes in the Church known as the Reformation.

The first English translations of the Bible appeared during Henry VIII's reign. At first Henry banned them saying that 'the word of God is disputed, rhymed, sung and jangled in every alehouse'.

When Henry died in 1547 his son became King Edward VI, and Parliament made him head of the Church in Henry's place. He was only nine so other people ran the country for him, and they carried on with the Reformation:

- Priests had never been allowed to marry; now they could do so.
- Churches were stripped of statues and finery; everything had to be plain and simple.
- A simplified prayer book had to be used for all services. It was in English instead of the old language, Latin. There were also Welsh and Irish versions.
- Ordinary tables had to be used instead of altars.

 A present-day historian wrote:

... at one Devon village the parishioners were so incensed that on the following day (after Whitsun, 1549) they compelled the priest to don his vestments and celebrate mass in the old fashion.

Henry VIII giving the authorised English translation of the Bible to Thomas Cranmer, the Archbishop of Canterbury. This picture appears in that Bible.

Key ideas

Parliament	Reformation
Protestant	Roman Catholic

A changing Church

Read the information on this and look at the picture of Henry VIII handing the Bible to Thomas Cranmer.

1. What would this picture have told people about the English translation of the Bible?
2. Why do you think this picture is in the Bible?
3. What did Henry really think of the idea of an English Bible? How do you know?
4. Do you think it was a good idea to have the Bible and Prayer Book in English instead of Latin? Explain your answer.

Some Tudor monarchs were Protestants and some were Roman Catholics, and each of them wanted the country to have the same religion as themselves. However, some people wanted to stick to one faith and not change to suit each king or queen. This led to trouble, especially when Edward VI died in his teens and his half sister Mary became queen. Mary's mother, Catherine of Aragon, came from Spain, which was fiercely Roman Catholic. Mary stuck to the Catholic faith, and she undid everything Henry and Edward VI had done to the Church in England:

- Married priests lost their jobs.
- Altars and statues were put back i churches.
- Services had to be in Latin, and all the old beliefs were restored.
- The Pope was head of the Church again.

Queen Mary curing someone of a disease called the King's Evil, by touching them.

Elizabeth, who followed Mary, brought back Protestant worship but she let Roman Catholics worship in their own way at home.

In Mary's reign several Protestant bishops were burned to death at the stake. This picture was drawn over 100 years later.

 Protestant and Catholic queens

1. Look at the portrait of Mary. What do you think the artist was trying to say about her?
2. Mary is sometimes called Bloody Mary. What does this suggest about the way she treated Protestants?
3. What does the picture at the bottom of this page tell you about Mary?
4. Which country might Elizabeth have feared? Why do you think so?

 People in Church

Read pages 28 and 29. Imagine you are an ordinary English person during Edward VI's reign.

1. Describe the changes that you would notice in church. Say which changes you like and which you dislike. Explain why.

8. Thomas More

A *Thomas More painted by Holbein*

There were people who felt that Henry was wrong to take charge of the Church. The most famous of these was a brilliant lawyer called Thomas More. With trouble brewing about his divorce, Henry appointed Thomas More as his Lord Chancellor – the most important judge in the country. Henry wanted More's help in getting round laws that stood in his way.

More was a scholar. He read new books as they appeared and took an interest in almost every branch of learning. At the start of his reign the King enjoyed his company very much indeed.

 According to More's son-in-law, William Roper:

The King used to send for Thomas More and sit and talk with him about astronomy, geometry, religion and other branches of learning. And on clear nights he would walk with him (in the open air) to discuss the paths, motions and behaviour of the stars and the planets. And because of his pleasant personality, the king and queen used to ask him to supper to hear his jokes.

 Besides his learning and good humour, More had a gift for understanding people's characters. When someone praised him for getting on so well with the King he gave the following sharp reply:

If my head would win him a castle in France he wouldn't fail to have it cut off.

 In the end, the King did turn against More, but More accepted prison and execution bravely, telling one of his daughters:

God, by this imprisonment, is making me one of his favourite children, bouncing me up and down on his knee.

B *The film* A Man for all Seasons *was about the life of Thomas More. This picture shows a scene from the film where Thomas More is on trial. More is on the right.*

Using evidence

1. Source **B** comes from a film about Thomas More called *A Man for All Seasons*. What do you think the actor and director were trying to say about his trial?
2. Look at Source **A**, which was painted while Thomas More was alive. What can you find out from it about him?
3. Do you think More is shown accurately in the film? Give reasons for your answer.

Thomas More was put in prison, found guilty of treason and beheaded in 1535. His life and death inspired and encouraged other people who wished to stay loyal to the Pope in Rome. In the years that followed Henry's reign, such people became known as Roman Catholics, while those who accepted change in the Church were known as Protestants.

More had thought of becoming a monk, and he spent part of every day in prayer. His conscience told him that the King was wrong to defy the Pope by divorcing Catherine and marrying Anne, so he gave up his job as Lord Chancellor. Two years later, in 1534, he refused to sign a document agreeing to Henry's control of the Church.

Catholic and Protestant

In large parts of Europe the Church stayed under the Pope's control. Elsewhere it broke away and accepted new ideas. The difference still exists today and was very important in Tudor times. Find out which parts of Europe are Roman Catholic and which are Protestant.

God's servant first

1. Who do you think spoke the words at the top of page 30?
2. Explain how they fit in with his life.

Key ideas

primary evidence   Roman Catholic
Protestant   secondary evidence

This royal infant,
Though in her cradle, yet now promises
Upon this land a thousand blessings which time
shall bring to ripeness.

9. Elizabeth I

The playwright William Shakespeare wrote the words at the top of this page. They appear in his play Henry VIII and they refer to Henry's new-born daughter Elizabeth who was born in 1533. By the time Shakespeare wrote these words Elizabeth had died at the age of 70, after a reign that lasted 44 years.

At the beginning of Elizabeth's reign her advisors tried to find a husband for her, but although she had many men friends, she never married. She said, when she was older, that she was 'married to her country'.

This is how a French visitor described her in 1597:

She wore a great red wig ... Her face appears to be very aged. It is long and thin and her teeth are yellow and unequal ... Many are missing.

This is how a German visitor described her in 1598:

Her face (was) oblong, fair, but wrinkled; her eyes small yet black and pleasant; her nose a little hooked; her lips narrow and her teeth black (a defect the English seem subject to from their too great use of sugar). She wore false red hair.

A *Elizabeth I painted in 1558, when she was 25.*

Trade brought foreign fashions and material to England and Elizabeth tried them all.

A messenger from the Scottish queen, Mary Queen of Scots, described a meeting with Elizabeth:

One day she had the English style of dress, another the French, another the Italian and so forth ... She delighted to show her golden coloured hair ... (and she wanted me to tell her) whether my queen's or hers was best ... I said she was the fairest queen in England and mine the fairest queen in Scotland.

Key ideas

fashion   trade

B *Elizabeth I aged about 15*

C *Elizabeth I aged about 65*

Elizabeth left over 3,000 dresses when she died. An inventory made just before she died listed her clothes. Here are some of them:

Bodices	85
Petticoats	125
Cloaks	96
Robes	99
French gowns	102
Loose gowns	100
Round gowns	67

 Portraits of Elizabeth

Look at the portraits of Elizabeth I. (Sources **A,B,C** and **D** over the page.)

1. Describe any changes in Elizabeth's appearance. Note anything unusual. Explain this.
2. Why do you think Elizabeth had so many portraits painted?
3. What do you think she wanted to tell people about herself by having portrait **D** painted?

 Comparing evidence

Read page 32. Look at Source **C**.

1. Draw Elizabeth as the French and German visitors described her. How are the descriptions different from the portrait of Elizabeth at that time? Explain these differences.
2. Why did the Scottish messenger not give Elizabeth a proper answer to her question?

 Inventories

1. Make an inventory (or list) of your clothes. What would this list tell people in the future about you?
2. What does Elizabeth's inventory tell us about her?

A female monarch

1. Elizabeth described herself as 'a weak and feeble woman'. Was she really weak and feeble? What evidence do you have to support your answer?
2. Why do you think Elizabeth said she was weak and feeble?
3. Why do you think it was difficult for a woman to be a leader in wartime?
4. Leaders often give stirring speeches in wartime. Why do you think they do this?

D *The 'Armada Portrait' painted in 1588*

During Elizabeth's reign, in 1588, King Philip of Spain sent a fleet of ships called the Armada to attack England.

Key ideas

conquer	Protestant
evidence	Roman Catholic
kingdom	warfare

Here is part of the speech that Elizabeth gave to her troops:

I have come in the heat of battle to live or die amongst you all; to lay down for my God, for my kingdom and for my people my honour and my blood, even in this dust.

I know that I have the body of a weak and feeble woman but I have the heart and stomach of a king, and a king of England too, and I think it foul that Spain or any prince of Europe should dare to invade the borders of my realm. I know you have deserved rewards and crowns; and I promise you on the word of a prince that they shall be paid to you.

We shall have a famous victory over these enemies of my God, my kingdom and my people.

You can find out more about the Armada in Chapter 12.

Queen Elizabeth giving the speech to her troops as the Armada was arriving.

As a young princess, Elizabeth was locked up in the Tower of London. Her half sister Queen Mary ordered her imprisonment in case the Protestants tried to make Elizabeth queen..

 A man who lived at the time remarked:

Her intellect and understanding are wonderful, as she showed very plainly by her conduct when in danger and under suspicion.

When Mary died and Elizabeth became queen she called it 'the work of the Lord' and said it was 'marvellous'. She avoided forcing her Protestant views on her subjects, and this helped to give England a time of peace and prosperity.

However, there was trouble with Scotland. In 1567, Protestant enemies drove Mary Queen of Scots into England, and Elizabeth had her put in prison. She feared that Roman Catholics would want to make Mary Queen of England, and several Catholic plots were discovered.

Some of the things Mary said showed what she thought of Elizabeth. One of Elizabeth's closest friends was a married man called Robert Dudley, whose job was to care for Elizabeth's horses. Dudley's wife died suspiciously, and Mary Queen of Scots remarked: 'So the Queen of England is to marry her horsekeeper, who has killed his wife to make room for her.'

Despite such suspicions, Elizabeth never married or had children, and this increased the worries about who would be the next monarch. However, Catholic hopes were dashed in 1587, when Mary Queen of Scots was put to death after twenty years in prison.

Secret messages

Mary sent letters from prison in a secret code, but Elizabeth's spies knew what was happening. Use the code to write a sentence that might have appeared in one of her letters.

a	b	c	d
○	‡	△	⊞
e	f	g	h
α	◻	⊘	∞
i	k	l	m
l	ȯ̃	l	//
n	o	p	q
∅	▽	ϸ	ɱ
r	s	t	u
ϼ	▵	Ɛ	⊂
x	y	z	
7	8	9	

 Dangers for Elizabeth

1. As a princess, how was Elizabeth in danger and under suspicion?
2. List three things that caused disagreement between Elizabeth and Mary Queen of Scots.

35

10. Court Life

A *Queen Elizabeth dancing with Robert Dudley, painted by Marcus Gheeraerts the Younger (1567-1635).*

A Tudor King or Queen had many attendants and servants. Some of the attendants were very important, wealthy people. They gave the monarch advice on matters like laws, taxes and foreign affairs, though Parliament made the final decisions.

Elizabeth chose a man called Sir William Cecil to be her Secretary of State – similar to a modern prime minister. Men like Cecil chose their own assistants and other staff, and this increased the number of people around the Queen. London had several palaces, and they all included separate homes for courtiers and their families, as well as rooms for men like Dudley, who cared for the horses, and rooms for servants.

Besides the Master of the Horse, the officers at Elizabeth's court included the Lord Chamberlain, the Lord High Steward and the Master of Revels.

 A man called Lord Herbert of Cherbury never forgot his first day at Elizabeth's court:

As it was the manner of those times for all men to kneel down before the great Queen Elizabeth ... I was likewise upon my knees ... when she passed by to the Chapel at Whitehall. As soon as she saw me she stopped and swearing her usual oath demanded, "Who is this?" Everybody there present looked upon me, but no man knew me, until Sir James Croft, a pensioner, told (her) who I was.

According to a witness:

Queen Elizabeth's temper was so bad that no councillor dared to mention business to her, and when even Cecil did so she told him that she had been strong enough to lift him out of the dirt, and she was able to cast him down again.

Another witness described how the Queen threw a slipper and hit one of her leading statesmen, Francis Walsingham, in the face with it. He went on to say that it was not a very surprising thing for her to do, as she was constantly behaving in such a rude manner.

B *Elizabeth I in her court painted by Frank Moss Bennett (1876-1953)*

Royal power

Think about what the witnesses' stories show about the Queen and her court.

1. The words at the head of this chapter come from a speech which Elizabeth gave to the House of Lords at the very start of her reign. How well did she stick to what she said? Why do you think so?
2. What do you think Elizabeth meant when she said she had lifted Cecil out of the dirt and could cast him down again?
3. How do you think Lord Herbert felt while he was on his knees? Why do you think that he and the Queen did not speak to each other?
4. What do you learn about Elizabeth from Lord Herbert's report? (You may have two or three things to say.)
5. Look at Source **C**. What does this tell you about Sir William Cecil? Explain your answer.
6. Compare Sources **A** and **B**. What do they tell you about the activities of the court? Describe the differences in mood between the two sources.
7. Notice the dates of the two paintings. Which is likely to be more accurate? Why?
8. Read what Paul Hentzner wrote about a visit to Elizabeth's court (page 39). How is it different from Lord Herbert's report?

Key ideas

court   monarch

C *Sir William Cecil (Lord Burghley)*

11. Elizabethans at Sea

A fleet at sea

An hourglass used for telling the time at sea

In Elizabeth's reign, the English began to compete with the Spanish and Portuguese in exploring the world and founding colonies. One colony, Ireland, was very near England, but English sailors also made voyages to North, Central and South America and they founded more colonies there.

Francis Drake and his cousins John and William Hawkins went on trading voyages. They left England with clothing and other goods to sell on the west coast of Africa. There they filled their ships with men and women to sell as slaves in the Caribbean, where Spanish settlers needed people to work their sugar and cotton plantations. Finally, they brought sugar and cotton back to England to sell. Every stage of each voyage included buying, selling – and making money.

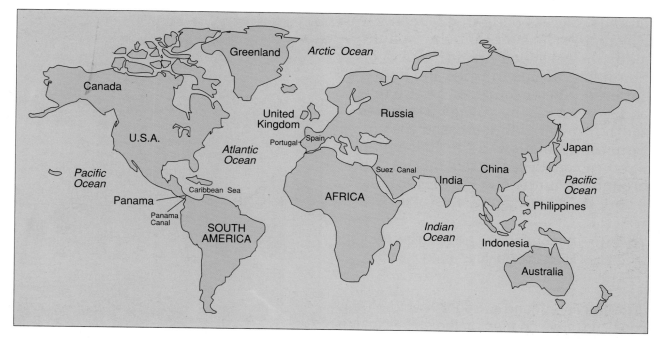

A modern map of the world

English and Spanish sailors robbed each other's ships. When Drake landed in Central America, in the area now known as Panama, he ambushed Spanish mule trains carrying loads of gold from one side of Panama to the other.

Key ideas

colonies   slavery
exploration   trade

England, Spain and central America

1. Look at the map and check the route of the voyages Drake and his cousins made. Make a very simple map of your own and mark the route on it.
2. While in Panama, Drake became the first Englishman ever to see the Pacific Ocean. Make sure you know where Panama is and how Drake could have seen the Pacific.
3. What route or routes would Spanish sailors travelling between the Pacific and Atlantic Oceans have had to use to avoid carrying goods across Panama?
4. Find out how the journey from the Pacific Ocean to the Atlantic Ocean was made easier at the start of the 20th century.
5. Look at the picture of ships. What problems might they have faced at sea?
6. How did sailors tell the time at sea? Explain any problems they might have had.

People on the move

1. Find out in which American countries people speak English, Spanish or Portuguese. How might sea voyages in Tudor times have affected the languages spoken there?
2. Imagine the scene when Drake bought slaves in Africa. With friends make up a short play about this.
   Think about:
   - the feelings of the slaves
   - their worries
   - what Drake's sailors said and did
   - how they agreed prices with slave sellers
   - language problems.

Drake's success delighted Queen Elizabeth. She said that she would gladly be revenged upon the King of Spain for various injuries she had suffered. She encouraged Drake to go on his most daring voyage. He sailed south from England, crossed the Equator and followed the eastern and western coasts of South America. This brought him into the Pacific Ocean, where he robbed Spanish ships.

 According to an English writer, Richard Hakluyt:

(The English) found a Spanish ship off the coast of Chile; the men on the ship, thinking Drake's men were Spaniards, welcomed them with a drum and a giant barrel of wine. But then one of Drake's men punched the Spanish pilot in the face and called him a dog.

Drake captured the ship and chained the men up. Then he went on shore and robbed the houses. He went into a warehouse and took the wine. He also took the silver dishes and the altar cloth from a little church.

Drake sailed right up the coast of southern and central America and half way up the coast of North America. He wanted to find a way back to Europe round northern Canada, but failed to do so. Instead, he decided to sail the rest of the way round the world. This meant crossing the Pacific Ocean and the Indian Ocean. Drake completed his return to Europe by sailing up the western coast of Africa.

Sir Francis Drake, painted in the 19th century by Samuel Lane.

The voyage took from 1577 to 1580 and some of his sailors died at sea. Most of them died from scurvy – a disease caused by lack of vegetables and other fresh foods. Sailors' gums bled, their teeth fell out and sores appeared all over their bodies. We know about scurvy from captains' log books and also from sailors' skeletons.

 Drake: gentleman or rogue?

1. Drake was a Protestant and he often held religious services on his ship. How did his religious belief make it easy for him to rob a church in a Spanish colony?
2. What does Hakluyt seem to think of Drake's actions? How does Hakluyt show his feelings?
3. Look at the portrait of Drake. Describe his clothes, jewellery and the way he is posing. What do you think the artist was trying to tell us about Sir Francis Drake?
4. Why does the artist show Drake with his hand on a globe?

 Key ideas

colony   Protestant

A modern reconstruction of the Golden Hind, *Sir Francis Drake's flagship.*

During Queen Elizabeth's reign another English explorer, Walter Raleigh, made expeditions to North and South America, returning home with tobacco and potatoes, which had never been seen in England before. Potatoes became an important crop in England and Ireland, and the English founded colonies in north America to grow tobacco.

Sailors' daily food ration was about 550 grams of biscuits and five litres of beer. They also had 550 grams of salt meat four days a week and fish on three days. On long voyages the beer turned sour and the salted meat and fish went bad. Sometimes ships' officers bought dried fruit, nuts and olives in foreign parts. At the ports, rats often managed to get on to the ships. They bred during the voyage.

 Life at sea

Read pages 40 to 43 and look at the map on page 41.

1. What dangers did Drake and his crew face? Why were they willing to face these dangers?
2. Describe anything you find surprising about the sailors' diet.
3. How do you think Drake managed to avoid scurvy?

 Using evidence

You can find out about the cargoes carried on Tudor ships from records of customs offices in large ports in England.

Court records and museums in large ports sometimes have records of items found on wrecked ships.

1. Find out as much as you can about cargoes carried on ships between 1550 and 1600.
2. Find out about life at sea for ships' officers and crews.

 The *Golden Hind*

Look at the photograph of the reconstruction of the *Golden Hind*.

1. How did the sailors defend themselves when attacked?
2. Describe any symbols or badges on the ship. What do they represent?
3. Describe the *Golden Hind*'s source of power.

12. The Spanish Armada

ORDERS,

Set dovvne by the
Duke of Medina, Lord general
of the Kings Fleet, to be obserued in
the voyage toward England.

Tranflated out of Spanifh into Englifh by T.P.

Imprinted at London by Thomas Orwin for Thomas Gilbert, dwelling in Fleetftreete neere to
the figne of the Caftle. 1588.

*The first page of a booklet in which the
Spaniards described their fleet of 130 ships.*

 King Philip of Spain prepared an armed fleet (Armada) of 130 ships to attack England in 1588. He gave this advice to his captains:

The English will want to fight at a distance, because of their advantage with cannons which they fire low to sink their enemies' ships – and because of the many artificial fires which they will have. The aim of our men must be to get close to the English and grapple with them.

 According to the English writer Richard Hakluyt:

The (Spanish) ships had everything needed on board such as carts, wheels, wagons, etc. They also had spades, mattocks, pickaxes and baskets so that settlers could quickly get to work. They had mules, horses and everything else a land army needed. They were so well stocked with biscuits that for half a year each man in the fleet could have half a quintal (25 kilos) every month ...

They had 147,000 casks of wine – again enough for half a year's voyage. They had butter and cheese, besides fish, rice, beans, peas, oil, vinegar, etc. On top of that they had 12,000 casks of fresh water and ... candles, lanterns, lamps, sails, hemp, ox-hides and lead to stop up holes. The Armada was reckoned by the King himself to contain 32,000 persons.

When the Spanish fleet was threatening England, most of Elizabeth's troops were at Tilbury, ready to deal with the Spaniards if they tried to land. The large, high Spanish ships moved slowly along the English Channel in a very close arrow-shaped formation and anchored near Calais.

 According to an English sailor:

The English took eight very old ships and sent them towards the Spanish fleet at two in the morning, with the wind and tide to carry them. When they had gone a good distance they were set on fire and left to float right to the King of Spain's navy. This fire in the dead of night put the Spaniards in such a panic that they cut the cables their anchors were joined to, raised their sails and took to the open sea in confusion.

Later, the wind gave the Spaniards new problems. Blowing from the south, it pushed the Armada northwards into the North Sea. With the English behind them they fled up the coast of northern England. They carried on northwards, even when the English turned back. They hoped to get back to Spain by going round Scotland and Ireland. A lot of the ships were wrecked but half got back to Spain.

Some of the Spaniards had been at sea for nearly a year. There had been little fresh food on the ships and many of the Spaniards had died from scurvy.

Key idea

conquer

 Attack

The English found out details of the Spanish fleet from the booklet which the Spaniards produced before the fleet sailed.

1. Find out from Chapter 11 why Philip II of Spain attacked England. You should find two reasons.
2. Countries usually keep their war plans secret. Why do you think the Spaniards produced the booklet?
3. Do you think we can trust all the facts and figures in the booklet? Why?
4. What do you think King Philip meant by 'artificial fires'? How might fire be used against the Spanish ships?
5. The Spanish ships were large and slow but how did the fleet appear strong? How did the English weaken it so that they could attack it?
6. Describe the journey of a ship that got back to Spain.

The route of the Armada

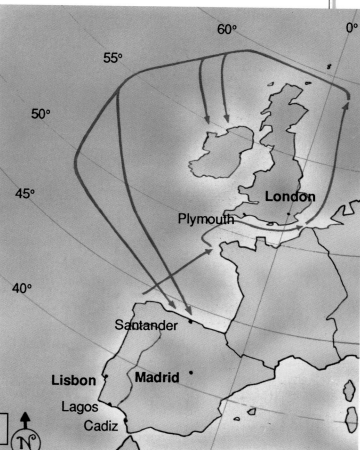

... can this cockpit hold
The vasty fields of France? Or may we cram
Within this wooden O the very casques (helmets)
That did affright the air at Agincourt?

13. Theatres

Until Elizabeth came to the throne there were no theatres. Small groups of actors travelled from town to town and performed in the courtyards of inns. People who were staying at the inn could watch free of charge from their windows and balconies. Other people paid to come into the courtyard.

We know about the buildings in various ways. There are clues in things that people wrote. William Shakespeare was one of the greatest playwrights in Queen Elizabeth I's reign, and the words at the top of the page come from one of his plays. They contain a very important clue about theatre buildings.

We also know about them from drawings people did at the time and from clues on the ground.

A *This inn in London still has the balconies where people watched plays.*

The theatres built in Elizabeth's reign had balconies round an open space, rather like inns. Wealthy people paid to stand or sit on the balconies; the poorer people paid less and they stood in the open space around the stage.

B *A 16th century drawing of a theatre in London*

C *William Shakespeare*

D *Excavating the Rose Theatre*

In 1989 archaeologists found the remains of the Rose Theatre, where some of Shakespeare's plays were performed. The floor was made of soil and cinders, and it also had lots of nutshells in it. It was very hard but something had damaged it in front of the stage. The archaeologists had to try and work out how this had happened. In the end they decided that the stage must have had a roof, and the damage was caused by rainwater running off it on to the ground.

The stage included a balcony. There is a 'balcony scene' in Shakespeare's *Romeo and Juliet*. Romeo was supposed to be calling from the street to Juliet's bedroom, so he used the stage and Juliet – played by a man – used the balcony.

Musicians also used the balcony above the stage, playing trumpet calls and other music to go with the action. The performers had costumes but not much scenery. Sometimes they put a wall, a bush or a throne on the stage, but the audience had to use a lot of imagination!

Watching a play

Using information given in this chapter, imagine the scene in a theatre during Queen Elizabeth's reign.

1. What refreshments would the audience be eating and drinking?
2. The lines at the start of this chapter mention a famous battlefield (Agincourt). Why will the audience have to use their imagination?
3. Discuss why theatres did not have a roof. What advantages and disadvantages did this have?
4. Look at Sources **A** and **B**. What does the design of the Tudor theatre remind you of?
5. Why do you think the remains of the Rose Theatre (Source **D**) were hidden for hundreds of years?
6. What do you think made it possible for archaeologists to examine them?

Key idea

archaeologist

Glossary

archaeologist
someone who studies the past from remains

baron
someone who owned a large part of the country

colony
an overseas land that people from another country take over

common land
land that is shared

conquer
defeat a land and take it over by military force

court
a group of powerful people that serve a king or queen

emblem
a symbol or badge

enclosure
fencing off shared land to be used privately.

exploration
sailing the seas to find new lands

export
selling goods to foreign countries

evidence
clues

fashion
popular style of dress

import
buying goods from foreign countries

industry
manufacturing or making things

kingdom
a country with a king or queen

leisure
free time

medicine
treatment for illnesses

merchant
a trader who makes a living by buying and selling things

monarch
a king or queen

monastery
a religious house for monks or nuns

mortality
the number of people dying

Parliament
people who decide on the country's laws

power
the ability to control people or a country

primary evidence
the first, most basic clues that are found: real objects such as artefacts, lists, or buildings

progress
advance. A monarch's tour around the land.

Protestant
a Christian who broke away from the Roman Catholic Church

recreation
time spent in enjoyment

Reformation
the founding of the Protestant Church in Tudor times

Roman Catholic
the Christian Church with the Bishop of Rome at its head

secondary evidence
clues worked out from primary evidence

slavery
owning people as servants

succession the rules about who becomes king or queen

trade
buying and selling

warfare
fighting between nations